Secrets for Finding
Happiness in Marriage

Secrets for Finding
Happiness
in Marriage

Valentino Del Mazza

Translated by Daughters of St. Paul

ST. PAUL EDITIONS

NIHIL OBSTAT
> Rev. Richard V. Lawlor, S.J.
> Censor

IMPRIMATUR
> ✣ Humberto Cardinal Medeiros
> *Archbishop of Boston*

ISBN 0-8198-6855-8 c
      0-8198-6856-6 p

Printed in the U.S.A. by the Daughters of St. Paul
50 St. Paul's Ave., Boston, MA 02130

The Daughters of St. Paul are an international congregation of Women Religious serving the Church with the communications media.

I dedicate these reflections
to all Christian wives and husbands,
to every woman and man of good will
and particularly to those who read this book,
that they may grow continually
in communion with their spouses
through day-to-day fidelity
to their marriage promise
of total mutual self-giving.

CONTENTS

The Art of
Conjugal Harmony

By natural law the most precious things are also the most fragile. If love is so beautiful that it is viewed as more divine than human, it is also true that the slightest error suffices to cast doubt on love and to weaken it. Marriage is like a boat carrying two persons in the midst of a stormy sea. A wrong stroke of the oars or an imprudent action on the part of one of the two parties is enough to make the boat capsize or even shipwreck. Love can also be compared to a crystal full of light; the slightest crack would be sufficient for the light to assume strange and amorphous proportions. Getting married is easy, but living together happily with a love which endures the trials of time is a lifelong art. It demands of the husband and wife the ability to know how to harmonize their lives for an ever greater happiness.

Because growth is essential to conjugal love, it may be helpful to suggest some norms which can be put into practice profitably by both partners, and then to offer some thoughts suggesting how a husband should build a positive relationship with his wife and vice versa.

1. Both husband and wife must *be committed* to conjugal harmony by feeling responsible for each other's happiness. The spouses must consider their union and communion as the first and irreplaceable occupation of their living together. Marriage is not an additional event in life; it *is* their life. Once Alexis Carrel, a French scientist and Nobel prize winner for medicine in 1912, was asked this question: "Is there something that all couples should take into account in their marriage?" "Yes," answered Carrel, "a very important thing: their marriage."

2. Conjugal harmony is an art which must be cultivated *starting from the wedding day itself.* It must be cared for, protected, educated, developed as the body is cared for until old age.

3. This technique of conjugal harmony is perfected above all *by practice.* A philosopher, John Lamarck, asserted that the mental and physical exercise of an individual determines his development and operational skill, while inactivity results in decadence. As one learns how to study by studying, to write by writing, to cook by cooking, to become a good athlete by continual exercise, likewise, the spouses perfect their living together by being continually

present to each other. It is rather encouraging to know that involuntary mistakes also can be instrumental in their improvement process. Mistakes, pains and quarrels are often the best means to regain or preserve conjugal love.

4. Both partners need much humility. When a husband boasts that he knows everything and is never wrong; when a wife has such a high self-esteem that she thinks herself indispensable and superior to all, certainly that couple's domestic peace is greatly compromised. A marriage can be considered successful when a husband and wife show mutual concern and a willingness to make up for each other's limitations.

5. Mutual understanding is based on reciprocal respect. Despite having many defects, it is always possible for a person to improve. Goodness and reciprocal love enable these virtues to shine like diamonds. The spouses must first of all consider each other's positive aspects and have more appreciation for what unites rather than what divides them. Their relationships will benefit greatly by a spirit of optimism. Who knows why so many couples wait until death to discover the virtues of their partner!

6. It is necessary to know the approach that leads to mutual understanding. There are some who, satirizing on marriage, would in-

sinuate that many couples go hand in hand on the wedding day, but misunderstand each other daily for the rest of their lives. To understand means to recognize one another's limitations in an exact and realistic way; to understand means to perceive some other motives behind sudden and explosive reactions; to understand means not to reject immediately one's husband or wife even though he or she did something wrong and had a bad day. To understand means to share enthusiastically the newness of every day as a gift from God.

7. Marriage is also a *call to patience.* Every little misunderstanding and motive of suffering should not be considered a tragedy. As every apprenticeship demands first an adjustment period, then flexibility and capacity of adaptation to the various situations, likewise love demands unfailing patience. Benjamin Franklin gave this useful suggestion: "Before marriage keep both eyes open; after marriage close one."

8. An eighth important rule for a deep union among the spouses is *the art of dialogue.* We have five senses: sight, hearing, touch, smell, taste; we are like a five channel television. Each one of us, however, has a preferred "channel" or sense. A husband, for example, may prefer to vivify his relationship with his wife through touch, while she may be inclined,

rather, to dialogue with him by word in conversation. Only if the two will be able to find and employ the wave of the best channel, without eliminating the others, will they find dialogue more easy and enjoyable.

9. Another efficient means in view of conjugal harmony is a willingness to *change our opinion* whenever it is clear that we are wrong. It is wise to acknowledge our own mistakes. To err is human, says a proverb, but to persevere in error is diabolical.

10. It is love that mainly decides the melodious symphony of two hearts. True love begins where nothing is expected in return. The fire of love is preserved only if it is nurtured, and it can be obtained only if it is consumed. Where there is no circulation of love, enthusiasm dies away; joy disappears; life is crushed. According to the well-known Austrian scholar, Victor Frankl, ninety per cent of the unstable marriages are the result of the egocentrism of one of the partners. What does it profit us if we possess the sun but do not share its rays?

What He Must Do for Her

1. The husband must be aware that his wife experiences the need to be esteemed and recognized in her *value and mission as a woman*. A legend relates that a young man went to knock at the door of his fiancée. "Who is it?"

asked a voice from inside. "It is I," answered the lover. "I don't know you," was the girl's reply. A year later, the young man tried again. "Who is it?" the girl asked again, hearing the knock at the door. "It is you," said the young man. "Now you may enter," the girl responded and opened the door.

2. Conjugal harmony demands of the husband a great respect for *the interior and spiritual side of his wife.* The feminine nature is a most sensitive recorder of facts and persons. A woman can suddenly become meditative and perplexed over the remembrance of a particular morning, an ill-fated day, a past sorrow, recalled even just by the tone of voice of the person speaking to her or because of the different manner in which someone gazes at her.

Pregnancy is an especially delicate period: she enters upon a cycle of hopes and fears; she sees herself different in the mirror and is conscious of the risks and sufferings awaiting her. In such circumstances, the husband should not approach her with the authority of a bronze-faced commander, but with delicacy, gently, in virtue of a love promised for a common joy. Flowers may be beautiful even without fragrance, but a fragrant flower is twice as beautiful. Likewise, a gruff husband may be good, but a good and gentle husband is twice a "treasure."

3. *A man should be grateful* to his wife for all that she is and for all that she does. A man could praise his wife in these terms: "You are the mirror in which I see myself; you are my heart, my life. You are the object of my happy hours, strength in my labors and hope in all my troubles. You are especially the 'wing' by which I can fly toward better things; you are for me the angel who carries me toward the light of God."

4. The husband must remember that the *woman is also concerned about fashion*, cleanliness and elegance. If man's temptation is the woman, the woman's temptations are the mink coat, jewels, lovely things. If she wants to be considered beautiful and keep herself that way, it is not so much to attract other men as it is to be superior to other women.

5. A good husband should be able to *love his wife also in little things*. The woman loves small details and wants to be the center of affection and attention, at least once in a while. It is a good thing for a husband to praise his wife for something well done, to recall her acts of virtue, to praise her successful deeds and personal accomplishments, to lay stress on the fact that without her his life would be without sunshine, enthusiasm and joy. Genuine courtesy is as creative as painting or music; by this classical means, man can always be the master

of his wife's heart. The woman! She is like the bee: well treated she gives honey; neglected and mistreated, she stings.

6. A husband should also show admiration for his partner. *Woman* by nature is *extremely romantic.* To be loved by her, it is not so necessary to say many things, as to whisper in her ear what she wishes to hear repeatedly. If she is beautiful, you don't need to tell her; it would be useless since she knows it very well. You should, instead, tell her: "Oh, how intelligent you are!" In case she is not so attractive, tell her emphatically: "Oh, how beautiful you are!" and she will think she has married a person with the soul of an artist. A *compliment* is something alluring for everyone. Once a little old man told a nurse: "How beautiful you are! How could God have made you so pretty?" And from that moment on, the old man was her favorite patient.

7. But even the most sublime words would be useless, if the husband would deprive his wife of his *presence.* One wife expressed in a very meaningful way this undeniable need: "It is an evening like all the others and I am waiting for him. I recognize the hum of the car motor, his way of stepping on the brake. Here he is; he stops to open the gate; the tires of the car shriek on the pebbles; the lights glide over the closed shutters of the house...; now he talks

to the dog, climbs the stairs, takes off his shoes so as not to wake me up. He walks in. He's home. Only now I feel like existing."

8. A delicate point concerning the duties of a man toward his wife regards *children*. A good Christian woman gets married to become a mother. Whenever a husband would purposely deny maternity to his wife, he would only injure the woman's very nature, weakening and emptying it of its significance. A husband who acts this way is either terribly selfish—seeking his wife only for himself almost as his slave—or he is affected by some psychological complex. And with the passing of time, he will be the one to suffer more damage. In fact, a woman can live by herself, at least as far as personal and economic autonomy is concerned, but only with difficulty will a man be able to cope with the situation, especially when he is old and sick.

9. It would not be at all inappropriate for a husband—we are still dealing with his duties toward his mate—to *ask pardon* whenever he realizes that he has done something wrong. The best remedy for a fault is to recognize one's own mistakes. Any time a man asks his companion's pardon, it is as though he has told her: "I offer you the occasion of loving and helping me. I really need you."

10. This behavior is not contradictory; rather, it fits the decisive leadership stance the husband must at times adopt to solve important or urgent problems. A woman is also very attracted by the firmness and steadfastness of the man. Although her nature is one of frailty and gentleness, by vocation, as the one called to the difficult task of maternity, the woman is endowed with strength and a self-giving spirit. In this framework, it is not surprising that she tends to be dominated and to dominate her husband, to be protected by him even in a resolute and explicit way, and at the same time to be his protector, light and guide.

Ten Suggestions for the Wife

To the duties of the husband correspond as many responsibilities on the part of the wife. It is fitting and right, therefore, also to set forth ten suggestions for her.

1. A woman ought to be aware of her power as a woman. A woman, Eve, brought ruin to the world, and another woman, Mary, brought joy to it. Man's future is the woman; history rests on the knees of the mother. If man performs feats, the woman reinforces man; if man is the head, the woman is that "neck" which makes the head move wherever she wants it to. From her—the woman—comes light and darkness, the sunset of beautiful things and

the dawn of many marvels. Aware of her twofold potential for good and for evil, each good woman should give herself to her husband in a spirit of service to contribute to his growth in the ethical, spiritual, and social dimension.

2. The husband also needs his *wife's presence*. Anthony Gramsci, an outstanding figure in the political and literary field, once wrote to his wife Julia Schucht, a Russian musician, who was rather indifferent to his fiery love: "My dear, I miss you very much; without you I feel immersed in a great void. I would like you to be with me, because my loneliness is a source of many worries and much sadness. It is as if I were suspended in the air, far removed from reality.... You must come back, my dear; I need you.... Anthony."

3. It is of paramount importance for a woman to acknowledge her responsibility to be the "sunshine of the family" and the "queen of the home." While it must be recognized that women have the same right as men to perform various public functions, they must feel bound to devote most of their time to their own families. If their stay outside the home were to become a continual and permanent situation, undoubtedly their home would be reduced to the role of a simple hotel. A husband continually needs material and moral support. This necessity creates in him the desire to return

home where he can find his wife ready to give him this assistance. A newly married man once shared this confidence: "Before marriage, I felt that I only existed, but now, when I go home and find my wife, I understand what it means to live." How great love is!

4. Because of this need of her partner, the wife, however, should not *enslave him*. Woman is possessive by nature and once she has found the ideal husband, she attaches herself to him like ivy to the wall. Like drops of water falling constantly on her husband's heart, her words, her requests, can often aim at making him do exactly what she wants and desires. A prerequisite of conjugal harmony is to leave the husband free to exercise his activities and hobbies. Love also means freedom for the loved one.

5. Another important thing a wife should always bear in mind is that a man is *more subject to nervousness than a woman*. Thus, when her husband comes back from the office or his work, he feels the need to relax and stretch out in an armchair. The wife should be aware of this and welcome him home warmly and with a smile. If, on the contrary, she were to immediately tell him of all the troubles of the day, the unpleasant things which happened to the children or of some other problems, she would just prepare the way for a quarrel which could even break out during the meals.

6. The woman should not immediately think evil if her husband tells her that he has a secretary who is charming and gracious. This is his way of relating a fact.

7. Every wise wife should have no trouble in being convinced that her husband, though unquestionably good and faithful, can be *very distracted*. Therefore, it would be good for every wife to bear in mind that if on a special occasion such as a birthday, instead of receiving a stronger manifestation of love and understanding from her husband, she finds that he is totally forgetful, she should not necessarily attribute this to ill intent and carelessness. It is usually only distraction. In this regard, psychologists offer this explanation: when a man is attached to his wife and loves her dearly, he no longer sees her as distinct from himself. This is why he is not so much concerned with showing attention.

8. The eighth rule of family harmony is this: *the wife should not make a tragedy of any small family disaster.* The home is not a bureaucratic system which complicates simple things, but a place of agreement where battles are fought together to overcome life's difficulties. Too often the wife develops a martyr attitude which could destroy the marriage and the family.

9. It is important to notice that man is weaker than he appears to be. Even if outside the home he is admired, esteemed and honored for his uprightness and accomplishments, *he feels the continual need of kindness,* sympathy, of being the center of his wife's affection. Even at the point of death he invokes her caress. If every wife knew how to instill in her husband the conviction that he is the center of all her attention, this would help him to be stronger, and more decisive, in a word, more of a man.

10. After all, it is only a question of understanding and practicing *true conjugal love.* A Spanish proverb says: "Everything is paid with money; but love is paid with love."

Love's Trials

All the beautiful things of this world cost labor and sacrifice. Love is a golden ring which, however, can mark the beginning of chains, that is, slavery. Getting married means entrusting one's life to another person whose being, like ours, is fickle, frail, not immune from oddities, perhaps even complexes, failings and even moral faults. Difficulties are created on a permanent basis by differences of character, education, mentality and different religious beliefs. To all this must be added the discomforts that result from poverty, unemployment, unstable economic situations, sickness, the death of dear persons, and misunderstandings even on the part of parents or others close to us. Above all, there can be an obscure social life. To complete the picture it must be mentioned that a specific crisis can arise after about ten years of married life or, according to some, in the seventh year.

At the root of this crisis is the fact that after some time together, during which the spouses have experienced and exhausted all the newness marriage has to offer, they are confronted with a reality which seems to become daily more difficult and monotonous. The increased awareness of each other's defects also contributes to creating an atmosphere permeated by uneasiness and dissatisfaction.

Some experts in this field maintain that this "mini-crisis" can have a negative consequence resulting from repeated, sentimental episodes experienced with stronger or weaker intensity between forty and fifty years of age. At this age, persons confronted with the difficulties of life and the hardships of marriage neither feel young enough to start a new love, nor so old as to remain within the narrow family environment and its strict moral code. To fill up their interior emptiness, therefore, they resort to erotic and sentimental adventures, compromising family harmony. Aware of this, the liturgy of the Church during the wedding, when the spouses pronounce their "yes," exhorts them to hold each other strongly by the hand as though wanting to convince them that only united can they better overcome the difficulties of life.

A Little Patience

Spouses must not think that only married life is beset with difficulties. Any road in life is bristling with obstacles. In order to evaluate their situation properly, couples should have lived and struggled in another walk of life. Even those who, for example, have obtained a divorce on the grounds of incompatibility and have entered into a new union, do not generally stop at the second conjugal experience, but go even further, resorting to a third or fourth marriage. This clearly evidences that life is always difficult for everyone.

It may help to think that life, in all of its aspects, has something hard to accept. Is it always a joy to live together with other persons in the office; in community; in our cities where we are surrounded by tension, haste, abuse, jealousy, self-interest, pornography?

Is it not perhaps a humiliation to have to accept laws more or less just and the conditioning factors which social groups, political parties or economic undertakings impose upon us? Moreover, every day we are bound to endure pains, sufferings, discomforts caused by the weather, the moods of the persons surrounding us, etc. Yet if, despite all this, we find love in our home, we possess much, or should we say, everything.

Difficulties in married life, considered from a positive point of view, will become more acceptable. Undoubtedly, those very difficulties might create a sense of dissatisfaction, but they are also precious means to pass from the emotional stage of love, as it is experienced during the engagement, to a mature love determined by the formation and growth of the will. If husband and wife have not experienced together some trials, if they have not suffered together for their family, they will hardly be able to grasp the true meaning of love. In fact, by virtue of a providential paradox, conjugal love is enriched by trials. It can be compared to the vine which produces better wine when growing in rocky grounds, or to the tree which strengthens its roots when being blown by the wind.

These considerations, however, should not lead us to the erroneous conception of a family immune from discrepancies. It is more than human and justifiable for husband and wife to get upset when faced with the tribulations of life and to have occasional verbal disagreements. But, in this regard, an easy way of overcoming each quarrel is available.

Ten Rules To Overcome Marital Quarrels

Here are ten rules aimed at fostering harmony in the midst of difficulties.

1. Husband and wife should not lose heart if occasionally they are at odds. *Quarrels in themselves are not negative signs regarding their love*, since obstacles are part of our human existence and are manifestations of the use of

our free will. If the spouses are so afraid of
every little incident or discrepancy arising
between them, they show that they love each
other very little.

2. *Husband and wife should be concerned
with always agreeing over essential things,*
such as religion, education of the children,
social relationships, etc., while enjoying freedom to express themselves freely about sec-
ondary things, such as fashions, amusement,
culture, etc. If husband and wife fail to be of
one mind and heart on essential things, they
have to draw the sad conclusion that their
marriage is only a contract between two iso-
lated parties. On the other hand, an argument
over accidental things, such as method, ques-
tions of time and space, may be profitably used
to develop a greater knowledge of life and a
deeper reciprocal love.

3. *Husband and wife should avoid arguing
in the evening when both are tired* and upset
due to the unpleasant things which occurred
during the day. If, in the evening, motives of
contrast arise or the discussion becomes too
"heated," it may be prudent to interrupt it by
keeping silence for example, or by resorting to
a "chronological compromise" consisting in
postponing the discussion of the problem until
the following day or on another favorable occa-

sion. Sleep has a therapeutic and prophetic power. It settles many things and heals many wounds.

4. *Husband and wife should never raise their voices.* He who loves less, yells the most as though he wished to make up for the poverty of his rational argument by screaming. Truth is not something which is thrown into someone's face. Rather, it is similar to a light which convinces merely by penetrating. The importance of this rule should not be underestimated since it is well-known that of one hundred quarrels, ninety are caused by the tone of voice, and a big quarrel implies the wounding of love.

5. It is a sign of intelligence to be able *to listen before answering.* Knowing how to listen implies humility, respect for the other, and especially love for one's partner. Listening is an art which enables us to answer according to truth and to avoid magnifying indefinitely the causes of friction.

6. When differences and quarrels arise, *it would be unwise to refer them to each other's parents.* St. John Bosco used to say: "Our rags should be washed by us, in our home."

7. *We should not pretend to be right at any cost, to win all along the line.* Let us learn from the animals which stop fighting the opponent after the surrender. All of us can be mistaken, and as John Jenkins, violinist and English

composer who died in 1678, wrote: "When the eraser wears out before the pencil, it means that we are exaggerating." Family harmony is so important that it cannot be compensated for by any verbal victory: "After a lost battle, the greatest misfortune is a battle fought to the bitter end."

8. Another rule which can be applied profitably consists in not shedding too many tears over things which are wrong but in trying, instead, to convert evil into good.

Already Socrates, in his own times, that is in the fifth century before Christ, used to say: "If you have a good wife, you will be happy, but if you have a bad one, you will become a philosopher and everyone will profit."

Taking leave of his students after they had received their doctorate, a university professor told them: "I wish you a happy married life; keep a book always within your reach so that when quarrels arise, you may simply take that book and read it. I assure you that you will acquire sure knowledge." On the other hand, a wife who is not fully understood by her husband can profit from her suffering by turning to Love "par excellence"—God's love, capable of fully understanding her. A renewed awareness of her limitations will also allow her to become as humble as the stars which are not ashamed to appear as small as fireflies.

9. After husband and wife have expressed all their motives of disagreement, they might benefit from laughing together so as to become convinced that, after all, what matters is to love each other. If one of the partners laughs, it may be said that the disagreement has resulted in understanding.

10. Finally, it must be observed that all the efforts to avoid or reduce quarrels will be ineffective without *a solid religious and spiritual basis*. This must comprise the virtues of goodness, sincerity, a spirit of sacrifice and forgiveness; the theological virtues of faith, hope and charity; the conviction that God sees and loves us. Only in this way will every contrast between husband and wife achieve a peaceful conclusion, since God is the solution even of those problems which apparently are unsolvable.

Sacrifice, Source of Genuine Love

From what has been said previously, we can derive the logical conclusion that true love cannot exist without sacrifice. To begin to love a person means to start a sorrow-filled life. "Cupid," that is, the Greek symbol of love, is portrayed armed with arrows to symbolize a love which produces bleeding wounds. The betrothed themselves experience this power of love under the influence of the classical thunderbolt when "she stares at him, and he becomes dumb" (Roman saying). Genuine love implies sacrifice since love means forgetting oneself in another, that is, a total surrender to the loved one to the point of immolation. One who loves little gives little, and one who loves much gives much, but one who loves totally offers the total gift of self. The "yes" that was pronounced on the wedding day is the beginning of a chain of numberless other "yesses" which bespeak abnegation and self-denial.

In this perspective, the daily tensions, the pains of living together, and the storms of life are occasions causing their love to pass from the romantic and sterile stage to the practical and oblative state, in imitation of Jesus Christ who has laid down His life for love of us.

This is so true that if a partner does not accept these conditions of love, but stubbornly wants to enjoy love as a reality conquered once and for all, or as a feast of a moment prolonged in time, then little by little love loses its strength, withers, dries up and fades away. On the contrary, a love nurtured by sacrifice becomes creative, practical, committed to that spiritual communion which is the mark of every authentic love.

There is a relationship between love and sorrow. We love truly that which makes us suffer. And we give ourselves with full awareness only in the hours of sorrow. Lovers know that nothing is higher and more fecund than a suffering they met and overcame together. It is in this setting that sorrow becomes the true generator of love because it is the only force capable of "divinizing" a word or a gesture. Only tribulation sets the soul free from the fever of the senses and transfigures it in the light of the love for the other. It is only after great sorrows that husband and wife look at each other with an affection they would never have expected, to the point of blessing that sorrow which has baptized them in fire.

It is necessary to suffer together to measure the quality of one's love.

Two Great Enemies of Love

The greatest dangers of all conjugal love are mainly two: divorce and abortion.

Here we will deal with only a few of the many effects resulting from these two evils. Guided by the love of truth and not by a spirit of polemics, we will share our reflections, prompted by a burning desire to promote what is good and honorable.

Divorce

When love is still in its initial stage, as during the engagement, everything is poetry, enthusiasm and sensitiveness toward the other. But after marriage even the most beautiful love may have its doubts, its weaknesses, its corroding worm. As a consequence, divorce may be resorted to and sought as a means of liberation.

First of all, divorce goes against love. The engaged couples repeatedly promise each other: "I will love you faithfully.... I will always be yours." The promise of an exclusive and unlimited love is a law of love. It must be noted, moreover, that the simple perspective of a possible marriage separation, not only would render false all the promises of loyalty made by the betrothed, but would endanger the very essence of conjugal love which tends to form only one flesh out of two. The simple thought of failure in such an important and indissoluble commitment would weigh on the joyous completeness of love.

Love is like a flower gradually stripped of leaves, which exudes from its petals a lasting fragrance. A deep and exclusive love between a man and a woman never becomes routine. True love is like a colorful plant rising from a lake; even if it is driven under the water a thousand times, it keeps coming out, fresh and bright, always more beautiful. Love endures forever.

Divorce Goes Against Common Sense

Marriage is a life spent together and embraced to better overcome life's difficulties. If only divorced people were able to understand this, they would not make a necessity or convenience of getting a divorce on account of the difficulties of conjugal life. On the other hand, it is the failings, the sufferings and the struggle of existence that enable the giving of self to the other; it is the negative side of a partner that constitutes the maturity "test" in love for the other. The desire of being always united, in good and bad times, in joys and sorrows, in victory and defeat, is for the partners an infallible sign of the truthfulness of their reciprocal love. To love without the giving of self is only a superficial sentiment of the heart. Love is worthless if it is always unwilling to help, to satisfy, to please the beloved one.

Another reason against divorce is the effect on the children. Everyone is aware of how the break up of a family affects children mentally, emotionally or psychologically. To grow and develop effectively, the ego of the child needs the constant and harmonious presence of his or her parents. Separated from one of his parents, a child is often prone to solitude, uncertainty and even to vice and crime.

Divorce Undermines Family Stability

Indissolubility is the principal source of a serious and mature family life. If stability in marriage is juridically damaged, how can a vocation of supreme ideals be established and fulfilled? The contrary will be true. The phenomenon of juvenile delinquency and drug addiction—are these not perhaps connected with the statistical increase of illegitimate children? And are not the percentages of suicides among the divorced three times greater than among married couples? And do not many other social crimes originate chiefly from psychically abnormal family situations? Strangely enough, attempts have been made for some years to heal society by disorganizing its fundamental nucleus and vital cell, the family.

Above All, Divorce Goes Against Life and Man's Perfection

If love were considered exclusively a biological and sexual force, it would be like turning on the motor of a car without being willing to put it into gear, or like sowing without wishing or expecting any fruit from the plant; that is, it would be like the denial of a complete love.

Love has varied ethical manifestations which can be expressed approximately in the following manner: at first, love is attraction, sex, emotionalism, romanticism; then, it is esteem, enjoyment of the partnership as in marriage. Later, love manifests itself in a stronger way as joyous and disinterested donation, as it exists between husband and wife in full maturity. Finally, as it is evidenced by the aged, love tends to reach the perfective stage of silent donation and sacrifice, even without the correspondence of the other partner. Once a husband told his wife: "See, my darling, every day I love you more and more: today more than yesterday and tomorrow more than today!"

A sixty-five-year-old husband said to an old friend of his: "You know, today I have celebrated forty years of marriage; yet I can assure you that it seems to me that I love my wife more now than forty years ago." The great French biologist, Louis Pasteur, dean of the studies on the causes of infective diseases, died on September 28, 1895, holding the crucifix in his right hand, and in his left, the hand of his wife, Marie Laurent, as a token of thanks for the perfection achieved by their love.

The Italian musician, Francis Cilea, passed away at Varazze in 1950. Before dying, he held on to the hand of his gentle wife, with untold tenderness, to express to her his gratitude for having cooperated with him for so long in a program of human, social and spiritual perfection. It is well known that when one of the spouses remains widowed, there is the realization of having become so united to the other as to desire ardently to be reunited with the dear deceased one as soon as possible. Love is not merely human, but bears already the vividness of eternity.

Finally, from the point of religion, it is useful to remember that faithfulness and indissolubility in marriage are signs of the love of God for humanity, and couples are called to participate truly in the irrevocable indissolubility that binds Christ to the Church His bride, loved by Him to the end.

Procured Abortion

Another evil which suffocates and extinguishes even the most beautiful and promising marital love is procured abortion. Unfortunately, the hedonistic atmosphere in which the young generation lives today, together with a pseudo-feeling of a universal brotherhood, have led to the depreciation of the Christian and ethical concept of the family, emptying it of its fundamental value: fecundity.

Abortion is the denial and defeat of life. Life is for everyone on earth a supreme good, a divine and unrepeatable gift. Health itself is certainly a most precious treasure, but it is not superior to life itself. The right to life is the first and most fundamental of all rights, and it must be respected at every stage of its development. To extinguish life means to poison the very spring from which we come.

Procured abortion is against love. Married love is the lamp enlightening the life of husband and wife. Abortion extinguishes this love, so much so that if a wife is forced by her mate to have an abortion, as a consequence, she will react psychologically by developing a sudden aversion for him. A woman is that much of a true wife as she is an authentic mother.

Abortion constitutes, above all, a humiliation for woman, on every level. The highest English medical authority, the *Royal College,* recently showed numerous consequences regarding the woman's health after an abortion: abdominal inflammation, fever, hemorrhages, possible perforations of the uterus and other later complications such as sterility, etc. (cf. "Abortion," by H. Van Straelen).

Because physical and psychological dimensions are strictly interrelated, it also follows that abortion can lead in the long run to the psychological disturbance of the mother. Some researches have reported a notable proportion of mothers who suffer emotional anomalies after the abortion. Many suffer, in one degree or another, from guilt feelings. Abortion, by violating womanly instincts, deeply embedded in the mother's personality, leads the woman to react against this guilt sense, showing often an aggressive attitude in support of abortion.

Abortion goes against society because "it destroys man" (John Paul II). The civilization of a people does not consist in technological progress or in war potential but rather in the cultivation of love. As Paul VI stated: "A sign of higher civilization is to retain the sacredness of the human institution, intact and holy. If we wish a more human society, we have to reaffirm the value, the dignity, the beauty of the life of all its children."

It is well known that centuries ago a notary had sexual relations with a girl named

Catherine. This unwed mother did not want to resort to abortion, and she gave birth to Leonardo da Vinci. In the nineteenth century, there lived in Bonn two sickly parents, who already had three children. When the mother became pregnant again, she did not want to seek an abortion. Instead, she gave birth to her child— Ludwig Von Beethoven.

Once, Cardinal Raul Silva Henriquez revealed confidentially: "If my mother had not been generous and had not said yes to the Lord after eighteen children, I would not be here." And St. Catherine of Siena, the insuperable witness of divine charity and human fraternity—wasn't she the second to the last of the twenty-five children of Iacopo and Lapa Benincasa?

Abortion is cowardice. Generally, the smaller and more defenseless a creature is, the more it deserves compassion and help from its fellow creatures. It is a law of nature in animals, and was already preached at the time of Christ by the pagans, as it is stated in the writings of Quintilianus, tutor of the grandchildren of the Emperor Domitian, in the first century A.D. A conceived child is at the total mercy of others who have to respect and help him if they don't wish to act cowardly.

Abortion goes chiefly against God. God has employed all His love and power as Creator and Father in creating a new human life, making it

His child; Christ died and rose to save this life
and to render it worthy of an eternal beatitude.
The Holy Spirit contemplates the joy of making
this soul His favorite temple. And now, all this
ineffable work of the Holy Spirit is contested,
blocked and nullified by the sinful "no" of
those creatures who, by vocation, should be the
first collaborators of God in transmitting the gift
of human life.

We recognize that maternity and paternity
are *always a risk*, a question mark. But life has
been given to make it fruitful, not just to live as
parasites. It is also important to bear in mind
that certain things which, under the influence
of the emotions, appear useful and true, with
the passing of time reveal themselves as sterile,
shocking and degrading. How many mothers
who resorted to abortion, thinking they were
doing well, today are sorry for their rash actions!

Christ spoke words which provide us with
a program: "The man who hates his life in this
world preserves it to life eternal" (John 12:25).
True love implies a courage which knows how
to suffer and to wait. Even the progress of
people toward civilization is not accomplished
by tyrants, but by the martyrs of love and
goodness.

As a conclusion to these considerations,
we would like to quote part of the speech given

by John Paul II during the Mass celebrated in Piazza del Campo, Siena, on September 14, 1980:

"The Gospel is a message of life. Christianity bears deeply in its whole content the sense of the value of life and of respect for life. The love of God as Creator is shown in this, that He is the Giver of life. The love of God as Creator and Father is shown in this, that man, created in His image and likeness as male and female, is made by Him a collaborator from the very beginning, a collaborator of the Creator in the work of giving life. To such a task is connected a particular dignity of man: the generative dignity, the dignity of father and mother, a dignity fundamental and irreplaceable in the whole order of human life—individual and social at the same time.

"The problem of the affirmation of human life from the first moment of its conception, and, necessarily also the problem of the defense of this life, is joined in a very strict way with the most profound order of the existence of man, as an individual being, and as a social being, for whom the first and fundamental environment cannot be other than a true human family.

"Therefore, the explicit affirmation of human life from the first moment of its conception under the mother's heart is necessary. Likewise necessary is the defense of this life when it is in any way whatsoever endangered (even socially!). It is necessary and indispensable, because in the final analysis we are dealing here with fidelity to humanity itself, with fidelity to the dignity of man.

"This dignity must be accepted from the very beginning. If it is destroyed in the mother's womb, it will be difficult to defend it, then, in so many areas and spheres of life and of human society. How is it possible, in fact, to speak of human rights, when this most primary right is violated? Today many talk about the dignity of man, but then they don't hesitate to trample the human being, when these present themselves, weak and defenseless, on the threshold of life. Isn't there a patent contradiction in all that? We must not tire of reaffirming it: the right to life is the fundamental right of the human being, a personal right that obliges from the very beginning.

"God, in fact, so loved the world as to give His only-begotten Son, so that whoever believes in Him may have life!...

"And God has so loved human motherhood, the motherhood of a Woman—of the Virgin of Nazareth, through whom He could give the world His only-begotten Son—that in this light all human motherhood acquires an extraordinary dimension. *It is sacred.*

"Life is sacred. And the motherhood of every mother is sacred. Hence the problem of the affirmation of life. The problem of the defense of life already in the mother's womb is, for all those who confess Christ, a problem of faith and a problem of conscience.

"And it is also a problem of conscience for others, for all men without exception: it is by reason of their very humanity."

Love Grows
and Becomes Incarnate
in the Children

Love is a sign of life, an opening to life, a projection on the future. Marriage is not the tomb of love, but the cradle of life; it is not a point of arrival but a point of departure for the expansion of the world.

Fecundity is the fruit and the sign of conjugal love, the living testimony of the full, mutual self-giving of the spouses. A child is the sign of conjugal maturity. A family without children is like a garden without flowers, a sky without stars, a picture without a frame, a song without a refrain. A man never feels so much that his mate is his wife as when he contemplates her as the mother of his newly-born child, and the wife in her turn never appreciates and loves her husband so much as when she considers him as the father responsible for the fruit of her womb. It is with the birth of a child that love expands and re-echoes creation, touching the heart of God.

Marriage and conjugal love are by their very nature ordained toward the *begetting* and *education* of children. Children are really the supreme gifts of marriage, and contribute very substantially to the welfare of their parents.

The more one gives, the richer love becomes; love is multiplied with its own gift; it is nourished with sacrifice. For this very reason, the happiest are those who have loved and sacrificed themselves for others. The multiplied community multiplies happiness. In the relatively large family, the child learns to love from an early age and, therefore, becomes aware that he, too, must give up something for his neighbors. In this way, the disposition to altruism grows in him. What is more, in these families the child does not suffer from loneliness, because he finds there the possibility of fellowship. Such parents know very well what happiness comes from children in spite of the worries they cause. They enjoy far happier moments than those parents who for the pleasure of some things prefer to remain alone or with an only child, in whom, generally speaking, selfishness will grow because he will remain concentrated on himself because he is alone.

The Christian conscience is always on the side of love and life. Recognizing, however, the objective and subjective difficulties that generous parents may meet with in accepting more numerous children, Vatican Council II laid down the principles of *responsible parenthood.*

Responsible Parenthood

In what does responsible parenthood consist? Vatican Council II reminds us that the spouses are cooperators with the love of God the Creator and are somehow His interpreters; it is for them in the last analysis *to decide, personally and together, on the number of children they are to have, so as to educate them properly.* This decision will be based, not on passing whims or selfish motives, but on a love that grows and matures, that seeks its own good as well as that of the present and future children, the good of society as well as that of the Church. Spouses should be aware that in their manner of acting, they must always be governed by a conscience conformed to the divine law itself, and should be submissive toward the Church's teaching office, which authentically interprets that law in the light of the Gospel (cf. *Gaudium et spes,* nos. 50-51).

The most important decision for married people—to have, or not have, more children—carries with it the *right and responsibility of deciding on the means.* Pope Paul VI, in *Humanae vitae,* restated the Church's teaching about birth regulation. He reaffirmed, in absolute terms, the *immorality both of sterilization and contraception.* Having stated the Church's position on the evil of abortion, he says: "Equally to be condemned, as the Magisterium of the Church has affirmed on various occasions, is direct sterilization, whether of the man or of the woman, whether permanent or temporary. Similarly excluded is any action, which either before, at the moment of, or after sexual inter-course, is specifically intended to prevent procreation, whether as an end or as a means" (no. 14). Pope Paul continues:

"If, then, there are serious motives to space out births, which derive from the physical or psychological conditions of husband and wife, or from external conditions" (no. 16), there are morally acceptable methods of birth regulation, which are compatible with a Christian philosophy of life and a Christian understanding of responsible parenthood. The Church has pointed to continence in the past. Continence has to be exercised today also: for instance, sometimes before and after the birth of a child and also at many other times, because no marriage can remain constant without sacrifice and renunciation.

The encyclical *Humanae vitae* names specifically *the practice of natural family planning as a valid means,* in which the conjugal relations are restricted to the sterile days. This is not contrary to morals because the use of the natural cycle never involves a direct, positive action against the possibility of life; artificial contraception always involves a direct, positive action against the possibility of life. Pope Paul commended the natural regulation of birth as a "discipline proper to the purity of married couples" (Humanae vitae, no. 21). Many who are practicing Natural Family Planning, even when they are experiencing difficulties, will confirm, from their own experience, the words of Pope Paul.

During the past twenty years, many couples from every stratum of society—educated, uneducated, rich, poor, cultured and less cultured— have used God's way of causing infertility in planning the size of their families. Natural Family Planning is within the understanding of ordinary people, even the uneducated. The sacrifices required by the method are not such as to destroy marriage, but, in fact, the use of this method has increased the happiness coming from the marriage in spite of these sacrifices. This can only be attributed to God's blessing on these couples who fulfill their sacrifices.

On the other hand, the use of immoral methods has been known to lead gradually, as Pope Paul predicted, to a loss of respect by the husband for the wife and to a feeling on the couple's part that she has become the object of her husband's satisfaction rather than "his respected and beloved companion" *(Humanae vitae*, no. 17).

The practice of periodic continence requires the help of divine grace which God never denies to those who ask it with a sincere heart. For this reason, Pope Paul urges married couples to make the efforts needed, supported by the faith and hope which "will not leave us disappointed, because the love of God has been poured out in our hearts through the Holy Spirit who has been given to us" (Romans 5:5). It is necessary to implore divine assistance by persevering prayer; above all, to draw from the source of grace and charity in the Eucharist. The couple must not be discouraged if sin should still keep its hold over them, but rather have recourse with humble perseverance to the mercy of God, which is poured forth in the Sacrament of Penance (cf. *Humanae vitae*, no. 25).

Some Rules About the Education of Children

The obligations of parents toward their children do not imply merely to procreate them, but to educate them and bring them up in the fear of God and in faith. Sound psychology has never ceased stressing that parents must be the first instructors of their children. Many dedicated parents feel this responsibility and carry out their educational role with love and a most admirable spirit of sacrifice.

To help parents in their arduous but rewarding task of educating their offspring, ten rules can be indicated; ten norms to help parents better focus on the method and meaning of an easy and successful way of forming their children.

1. *Parents, refrain from giving your children all that they ask for.* Otherwise, they may grow up with the conviction that the world "owes them a living." For children, the greatest misfortunes in the world are mainly two: to

have nothing or to have everything. Someone once said: "Children are not vases to fill, but lamps to light."

2. *Avoid doing what your children can do.* Teach them to take responsibility. Thus, they will not easily shirk their family and civic responsibilities.

3. *Never quarrel in their presence.* If their home is not inviting, they will prefer to stay outside of it.

4. If the children learn to repeat some bad words, *do not laugh;* they may think they are funny, amusing, no matter what they say. It is the gift of speech, among other things, which distinguishes human beings from animals.

5. *Always be of one mind* in the parental decisions you make about your children; if they see you disunited, they will enter between you as conquerors siding with one or the other, as the small political parties do.

6. Do not wait until your children are eighteen *to speak to them of God.* Would you begin to send them to school when they are already grown up? Friendship with the Lord is the desire of all innocent children.

7. *Be single-hearted* in giving good example to them. When we love, we do not just talk well but rather live well. "You must act like the Child Jesus," a mother and father once said to

their child. "Yes," answered their son. "But when will you be like Joseph and Mary?"

8. If your children do something wrong, *do not humiliate them*, but encourage them to do better in the future. If you think of your children as endeavoring to master their destiny, you will be inspired to a sense of reverence.

9. Even if your little ones are refractory, impertinent, bad, *do not despair*. There are powerful energies of goodness and virtue in every child. As Boys' Town's Father Flanagan put it, "There's no such thing as a bad boy." At times it is enough to show these young people understanding, love, sacrifice, intuition and true friendship in order to arouse in them new orientations of light and promise.

10. *Always be serene friends of God* before your children, showing to your "treasures" that Christ is the Author of all freedom. Saint Catherine of Siena wrote: "In order to give freedom to man, and make him free, the spotless Lamb gave His very self to the disgraceful death of the most holy cross. See the ineffable love that with death has given us life. Bearing disgrace and insults, He gave back honor to us. With His hands bound and nailed to the cross, He has freed us from the bonds of sin" (Letter 20). "...With His death He has reconciled man with God: because the nails were made a key for us that has merited eternal life" (Letter 184).

Keeping Pace
with Others in Society

Love is too great and noble to be possessed and enjoyed totally only by a few persons and in a brief span of time. Love is a good which tends to communicate itself. The family is like a lens gathering the rays of love to project them outside to many others. Living, therefore, in and on behalf of society is the vocation and mission of every family, the first and vital cell of society itself. How could a person carry to his office, to his work, to his professional and political commitment, a community spirit of collaboration, if he had not developed it first in his own family? For this reason, Sophocles, a Greek tragedian of the fifth century B.C., wrote: "He who is good with his family is also a good citizen."

It is well known that society will be as strong as the individual families in it are. Every form of social and communitarian living together is like a construction; the individual stones or cement blocks are the families. If there are good families, if there is harmony in our homes and worthy projects are carried out together, families will undoubtedly have a favorable impact on the well-being and peace of the country. Here, too, a method is needed. Under this aspect, a series of reflections, which aim at making conjugal harmony flow into social harmony, may be useful.

Some Rules for Right Social Living

1. *Accept people as they are* and not as we think they should be. They are more weak than bad, more confused than malicious.

2. *Be unafraid* of telling others what we think is worth saying. The greatest misunderstandings in society, the gravest misfortunes which can befall a family or a community, are often caused by our unjustified and selfish silence. The word is a powerful instrument of light, solidarity and truth.

3. It is important, however, to *weigh carefully our way of speaking.* Avoid acting in a confused or arrogant way. Often, although we are right, we may be wrong in the approach we use. Above all, never flatter anyone. There is a difference between compliments and adulation: the former is a truth clothed in gallantry;

adulation is an open lie, as for example, when we tell a lady of fifty that she looks like she is twenty.

4. *Do not impose our ideas,* our tastes, but present our opinions with politeness and tactfulness. Do not monopolize dialogue as though truth were our sole right. Keep the promises we have made; forget the offenses; remove any rancor; continue to cultivate good friendships which are "the flower of charity."

5. *Be kind* with everyone, even with displeasing persons and those who are inferior to us in responsibilities or position, in learning or culture. St. Bernardine of Siena, a famous preacher of the fifteenth century, gave this wise advice: "Toward superiors we must show respect and docility, toward inferiors meekness, and toward the poor great evangelical compassion."

6. *Never murmur against anybody.* Speaking evil of anyone who is absent is meanness and cowardice. Criticism hurts the one who is responsible for it, the person who listens to it, and the one who is the object of it.

7. *Know how to listen* to those who would like to confide in us or tell their troubles. To know how to listen is something "divine."

8. *Take care to correct gently* those who might have done something wrong, choosing

the most suitable moment to do this and apologizing when we realize we have offended anyone.

9. *Greet those we meet*, possibly calling them by name. A greeting does not cost anything and is instrumental in establishing a good relationship with our neighbor. An impersonal greeting lacks compassion and warmth. Love is made of small things; it is simple as the light, vital as the beating of the heart, a reflection of who God is.

10. *We must endeavor above all to spread joy around us.* To the youth of Siena, Pope John Paul II said: "Christian joy is the distinguishing mark of the Christian, the song of the redeemed, of the new covenant, of brothers dwelling in unity.... There are youths like yourselves who have not found it; there are busy men and women who do not have the time and spirit to seek it; there are sick people in hospitals and elderly in homes who suffer from abandonment and loneliness. All these sisters and brothers await a smile from you, a word from you, your help, your friendship, and your handshake. Do not deny anyone the joy that comes from such gestures. Thus you will bring comfort to them together with benefit to yourself, because as Sacred Scripture says: 'It is more blessed to give than to receive' (Acts 20:35)" (Address to young people of Siena—September 14, 1980).

Faithfulness to God,
Source of Every Love

The family is the springboard of love considered in all its dimensions. Love is similar to a plant; it has its roots in the depths of man; overcoming all resistance, it emerges on the surface, seeking another love; it produces fruits—the children—and continues to rise to such heights as to border almost on the infinite. It suffices to complete the topic saying only that to love one another does not mean to complete each other reciprocally. It means that husband and wife look together in the same direction, toward God. A love which has nothing divine is merely the "eros" described by the philosopher, Plato, which knows not where it goes, and loves without knowing the ultimate and definitive reason of its donation. True love does not live only for the present but also for the future.

God Is Awaiting Us

According to the Christian ideal, marriage is the renewal of the covenant between God and the children of men. Each family is fully authentic and well established if it is based on a human love which has God's friendship as its foundation, nourishment and fulfillment. To love and be loved by God is like an exchange of kisses between heaven and earth. The sacrament of marriage is so great that it can be compared to the Eucharist. As Jesus gives Himself to us in body, blood, soul and divinity, so the spouses in their mutual giving of self can meet with the presence of God, hidden and efficient in each genuine oblative love.

God awaits us because human love continually needs divine love. Marriage is often a heavy burden which can be borne if husband and wife rely on the help of the Lord. Without divine assistance, conjugal love is like a safe full of treasures which cannot be opened because its key is lost. God is the source of every security, fecundity, harmony. God is not under us as an emergency net, nor above us as a protective roof, but within our spirit, giving us

strength, hope and comfort in every circum-
stance, even the most sorrowful. It is God's
style to recover things which are lost or worn
out so as to renew them and make them even
more beautiful. The true nuptial faith keeps the
couple united in love. It must constantly draw
vital lymph at the source of Him who estab-
lishes, builds up, renews, fortifies every rela-
tion of total love—the Lord.

St. Augustine, in one painting, is depicted
with the heart at the center of his body because
of his great insights into the divine Love; this
gives a very meaningful description of the
liturgical nuptial ceremony of his times. He
related that after the celebration of marriage,
the newly-married Christian couple was saluted
by a storm of applause, because with the
freshness of their love, husband and wife
would contribute to the joy and increase of the
Church, and because they had made themselves
available to the reception of divine grace. Truly
the Church is not only a greater sign of the
conjugal love between man and woman, but she
is also a source of divine help for the events and
the noble conquests of each marriage.

How To Draw Strength and Hope

There are two things in the world we
cannot do alone: get married and be Catholics—
that is, be in the Church and walk with the

Church. From the Church the spouses learn how to accept the *Word of God* that it may show them the right path in their daily life and on their pilgrimage toward the Absolute. Married life needs this Word of God which gives light to the mind.

The sacraments. Human sentiments, even the loftiest, can wear away. For a moment, straw can produce a lively flare-up, but it turns soon to ashes. Strong and uninterrupted stocks are demanded to feed love unceasingly. The Church understands the problems confronting the spouses and she reaches out to them offering the riches of her sacraments. They do not modify the earthly and human realities of the spouses, but only their interior and supernatural realities. The power of the sacraments can be compared to the sun, whose heat benefits the vineyards of the earth, though there is a great difference in the wines produced. The sacrament of marriage reserves a special grace for those willing to make of their love a continual song of harmony and joy.

Prayer. Prayer is greatly needed to preserve a harmonious love immune from infidelity. The Christian family achieves fulfillment when husband and wife pray together, encounter each other, reach out to one another and are united in the greatest love in the world, the love of God. Jesus says: "Where two or three are gathered in my name, there am I in their midst"

(Matthew 18:20). Catholic couples, therefore, must find time and the way for some prayer in common, even having one of their children lead the prayers. John Paul II, taking inspiration from an exhortation of St. John Chrysostom, has often repeated that each Christian family should be a "mini-Church." The moment we stop praying, we begin doing wrong things. On the contrary, by praying we obtain vital wisdom, divine strength and the possibility of communicating with the Eternal. Every successful marriage is the union of two hearts with God in their midst. Every couple can pray:

We thank You, Lord, for having united our souls in the profound joy of an authentic human and Christian love.

Render us worthy of this love, so that in the indissoluble union of our lives we may never lose sight of the ultimate end for which we are united.

Grant us a deep, delicate, serene, faithful, lifelong love, a sweet love, at times exciting but never whirling or oppressive.

Make us humble and recollected, that we may heed Your voice and proceed without presumption and pride in the way of perfection.

Put in our hearts, Lord, a burning desire of pleasing You always, of living for You, of practicing Your charity everywhere, despite the inevitable crosses of life.

May we generously collaborate with Your plans of love, willingly receive, educate, sacrifice ourselves for the children You will entrust to us.

Grant us a love not limited to the selfish enjoyment of our home, but open to all the brothers in service and truth.

Help us, Lord, to will what is pleasing to You; to be faithful to Your promises and to that wonderful design of goodness You have for each one of us for Your glory and for Your joy.

Grant us, finally, to possess, always and everywhere, that peace You have promised to all persons of good will, as a prelude of the eternal happiness of heaven.

Song of Joy
in the Home

Under this perspective I do not hesitate to affirm that conjugal love and joy are interdependent realities. Joy postulates a companion; laughing alone is only half laughing. One of the greatest joys in the world derives its origin from that mutual love nourished by hope that the partners exchanged on the wedding day and will continue to exchange generously throughout their lives. True love—that proclaimed by Christ—is creative, and each creation carries within itself a good amount of joy. Love is donation and each gift is a symbol of life and happiness. Love is life, and each emission of energy usually implies freshness and brightness of joy. If one loves only superficially, sexually or genitally, reducing love to a fleeting exchange of selfish sensations, there can only be a manifestation of pleasure, but not true joy. The "snack bar" of love, that is, the seizing, in an exclusive way, of its minutest pieces, on a simply emotional level, does not fill the soul with happiness, but rather empties it. Only when love is total and involves the whole person, does the husband-and-wife relationship really become a festival of true joy, and the family a monstrance of happiness.

For this reason husband and wife will always aim for a home of their own, the ideal of every love. It is here, in their own home, that spouses can develop the virtues of self-mastery, self-discipline, generosity, patience, the spirit of adaptation, collaboration and sacrifice. The home is the place of projects and hopes, of understanding and mutual enthusiasm; here true equality is realized without legalism or uniformity; here true freedom is sanctioned in view of common values and in virtue of loving intuitions; here, in the home, there is the possibility of becoming mature persons, fulfilled in body, spirit and soul. It has been said that the young English general, Arthur Wellington, who defeated Napoleon at Waterloo on

June 18, 1815, on his way back home, ex-
claimed: "It is here that I won my battle!"

A home is also a place of peace, the shelter
from every social injustice, contrast or disorder.
When there is security and harmony within the
home, everything is beautiful and bearable even
if outside its walls there is noise and contradiction. When love between husband and wife is
based on lofty sentiments, it can cope with
every adventure or every drama of modern life.
Unfortunately, today, in factories, in offices, on
the buses, trains and planes, many anonymous
and unknown people are met who are wounded
and oppressed in their hearts by what John
Paul II calls: "a metaphysical solitude." Many
persons go through the roads of the world
closed up in those metal boxes called "cars,"
almost suffocated, lost in the traffic after many
distressing experiences. It is only in one's home
that there remains the possibility of restoring
oneself in body and spirit, of regaining taste for
life, the value of existence. It is here in one's
home that love can almost miraculously regain
its identity and restore to our spirit that joy we
all long for. It is so! A home can replace the
entire world while the entire world can never
replace a home.

Ten Beatitudes
for Christian Spouses

As a synthesis of these reflections, it seems fitting to offer ten beatitudes for Christian spouses.

1. Blessed are those spouses whose principal ideal in life is the fulfillment of their *union on all levels,* making of their house a little church in the kingdom of God.

2. Blessed are those spouses who in the Sacrament of Matrimony see a new *style of living,* acting, understanding and enriching their own soul, their own experience.

3. Blessed are those husbands and wives who, in the name of God, make of their love a continual occasion of exchanging their thoughts, their expectations, their hopes, their sublime and worthwhile programs.

4. Blessed are those spouses who, aware of the impact of evil and sin, refrain from watching bad or objectionable shows and avoid all that can obscure the genuineness of their understanding and collaboration in doing good.

5. Blessed are those spouses who, on the "evening" of their earthly journey, know *how to pray together*, entrusting themselves to that divine Love, who was at the beginning of all their nuptial joy.

6. Blessed are those spouses who are not averse to being *"co-creators with God,"* giving with trust and generosity, life to their children—who are the hope of society and the Church.

7. Blessed that family in which the *Gospel* is read and meditated on as the only valid code of life, on which one's own thoughts must be examined and individual actions must be carried out.

8. Blessed are the husband and wife who in moments of trial and mourning know how to *suffer together*, supported by that "Hope which does not disappoint" (cf. Romans 5:5).

9. Blessed are those spouses who sanctify the feastday as a time of life and recovery to strengthen and adorn, evermore, their consecrated love.

10. Blessed are the husband and wife who know how to sacrifice themselves for each other's joy, because both direct their love toward the eternal love of the Father!

A Message

As a conclusion to this friendly conversation, it may be appropriate and useful to report the message that the Holy Father, on October 12, 1980, the day dedicated to families, delivered to the special audience attended by the representatives of about sixty Church family movements. Pope John Paul II said:

"We have all followed with emotion and gratitude the words of those who have wished to bear their real-life witness here. They were short narratives, which, however, enabled us to catch, behind the necessarily concise sentences, a glimpse of real poems of love and dedication, the individual chapters of which we will get to know thoroughly in the kingdom of God, and this, too, will be part of the perfect joy of that time. I am sorry not to be able to take up again and develop all the subjects which have been recalled here with the liveliness, the freshness, the forcefulness characteristic of all testimonies rooted in personal experience.

"I cannot pass over in silence, however, the appreciation with which I listened, for example, to the two young fiancées speaking of the priority they had given to spiritual values over material ones, in the preparation of their marriage. And in the same way I was struck by the clarity with which stress was laid, in the various testimonies, on the positive impact that the commitment to live love chastely had on its growth and its development. In the midst of so many voices which in our permissive society exalt sexual 'freedom' as a factor of human fullness, it is right that there should also be raised the voice of those who, in daily experience of serene and generous self-control, have been able to discover a new source of mutual knowledge, deeper understanding and true freedom.

"I also noted with deep joy that the various couples showed that they felt it a 'natural' requirement of their love to be open to brothers, in order to offer to those in need understanding, advice, and concrete aid: the altruistic dimension is part of true love which, giving itself, instead of becoming impoverished and dispersed, finds itself enriched, enlivened and strengthened.

"A fact that emerged in the various experiences presented was the awareness, perceptible in the words of all, that true love is the key to solving all problems, even the most tragic ones, such as the failure of the marriage, the death of the partner or of a child, the war. The way out— it was said—is always and only love, a love stronger than death.

"Human love is, therefore, a frail and menaced reality: everyone recognized this, explicitly or implicitly. To survive without drying up, it needs to transcend itself. Only a love that encounters God can avoid the risk of losing itself along the way. From different standpoints, those who spoke bore witness to us of the decisive importance that dialogue with God, prayer, had in their lives. In the experience of each one there have been moments in which it was only through God's face that it was possible to rediscover the real features of the face of the loved one.

"These are some of the beautiful things that these brothers and sisters of ours said to us today. We are grateful to them because now, after listening to them, we feel richer.

"We are fully aware, in fact, that we have a lot to learn from those who are trying to live consistently the unfathomable riches of a sacrament. It is in the wake of the testimonies that we have just listened to that I want to express some thoughts of mine now, pursuing, as it were, a dialogue.

"And first and foremost I am anxious to say: it is necessary to restore confidence to Christian families. In the storm now raging over it, under indictment as it is, the Christian family is more and more tempted to give way to discouragement, lack of confidence in itself, and fear. We must, therefore, tell it, with true and convincing words, that it has a mission and a place in the modern world and that, to carry out this task, it has formidable resources and lasting values.

"These values are, above all, of a spiritual and religious order: there is a sacrament, a great sacrament, at the root and at the base of the family, a sacrament which is a sign of the active presence of the risen Christ within the family, just as it is also an inexhaustible source of grace.

"But these values are also of a natural order: to illuminate them when they are dimmed, to strengthen them when they are weakened, and to rekindle them when they are almost extinguished, is a noble service rendered to man. These values are love, faithfulness, mutual help, indissolubility, fecundity in its fullest meaning, intimacy enriched by opening towards others, the awareness of being the original cell of society, etc.

"The family is the steward and privileged transmitter of these values. The Christian family is so in a new and special way. These values strengthen it in its being and make it dynamic and efficacious in the community as a whole at every level. But the family must believe in these values, it must proclaim them fearlessly and live them serenely, transmit them and spread them.

"My second thought is this: the more the 'passion' of the family in the conditions of our modern world is extensive and takes on varied faces (we perceived this clearly on listening to the testimonies!), the more universal must be 'compassion' for the family.

"What, therefore, is the Christian family suffering from today? It is suffering, of course, in poor countries and in the poor areas of rich countries; it is suffering serious harm from regrettable situations of work and wages, of hygiene and housing, of food and education.... But this is not the only suffering: even the well-to-do family is not protected from other difficulties. The difficulty that comes from lack of preparation for the high responsibilities of marriage; that of misunderstanding among members of the family, which may lead to serious breaks; that of the deviation, in various forms, of one or several children, etc....

"No man, no human group alone can remedy these different forms of suffering. That calls for the commitment of everyone: the Church, the states, intermediary bodies, the various human groups, are called, in respect for the personality of each one, to effective service of the family. Above all, the commitment of each of the spouses is necessary, and, for this purpose, it is greatly to be hoped that husband and wife have—or endeavor to have—from the outset, the same view about the essential values of the family.

"A last thought brings me to an invisible dimension, which cannot be expressed in numbers, but which has to be considered among the most important, if not *the* most important one of the family reality. I am referring—you will have already guessed—to family spirituality. All considerations on the Christian family should always converge towards this reference point as towards their own root and their own summit. In fact, the Christian family springs from a sacrament—that of marriage—which, like all sacraments, is a bewildering divine initiative at the heart of a human existence. Then, too, one of the purposes of this sacrament is to construct with living cells the Body of Christ which is the Church. The family can be understood only in the field of attraction of these two poles: a call from God which is binding on each one of the Christians who compose it, the response of each one in the great community of faith and salvation on its pilgrimage towards God.

"Nevertheless, a Christian family embodies and lives all this in the context of elements which belong specifically to the family reality: human love between husband and wife and between parents and children, mutual understanding, forgiveness, reciprocal help and service, the education of the children, work, joys and sufferings.... All these elements, within Christian marriage, are enveloped and, as it were, impregnated by grace and by the virtue of the sacrament, and become a way of evangelical life, a search for the face of the Lord, a school of Christian charity.

"Then there is a specific form of living the Gospel within the framework of family life. To learn it and put it into practice is to live marriage and family spirituality fully. In the hour of trial and hope that the Christian family is living, it is necessary for a larger number of families every day to discover and carry out a sound family spirituality in the midst of the daily fabric of their own existence. The effort made by Christian couples who, inside or outside family movements, endeavor to spread, under the guidance of enlightened pastors, the main lines of a true marriage and family spirituality, is more necessary and providential than ever. The Christian family needs this spirituality to find its balance, its complete fulfillment, its serenity, its dynamism, its opening to others, its joy and its happiness.

"Christian families need someone to help them to live a real spirituality.

"These are some considerations by which I set particularly great store. I entrust them to you and invite you to study them more deeply through personal reflection and in common conversation with your partner, and to draw suitable conclusions from them for yourselves and your married and family life. Always be aware that as a Christian family you are never alone and abandoned with your joys, needs, and difficulties. In the large community of the faithful many other families are walking at your side: your pastors and bishops assist you, by order of Jesus Christ, and the Pope, too, thinks of you in tireless pastoral concern, and prays for you in love of the Lord.

"In this vast brotherly community of the Church, I therefore greet in you also all married couples and families in your respective home-lands, for whom it was impossible to take part personally in this Day of the Family. We are sure that they too have participated, individually and with the members of their families, in today's worldwide prayer of the Church for the family. We have prayed here at the center of Christendom for them, too, and for all families in the world. We feel united with them in the same way and pray for the special protection and assistance of God for them as for all the families represented here.

"Many families from my country, too, are taking part in today's unusual meeting, characterized by the dimension of a testimony, before God, the Church and the world, to the Christian family and its tasks in the modern

world. And this gives me particular joy. I
welcome you and cordially greet you all at
St. Peter's tomb, at the heart of the Church. In
you, present here—and through you—I greet
every Polish family, both in the homeland and
outside its frontiers: every father, every mother,
every child who is the hope and the future of
the world and the Church. Take this greeting
and my blessing to the thresholds of every
home, to every family. And also take this
experience and this testimony of the family
which you have given here in Rome, and those
that the Church gives on the family.

"From Rome, from the present Synod of
Bishops, and from all that you are experiencing
in the course of these days, you draw the
conviction, the confidence, and the certainty
that it is a right and duty of the Church to
cultivate and carry out her doctrine in pastoral
guidance on marriage and the family.

"She does not intend to impose this doctrine and guidance on anyone, but is ready to
propose them freely and to safeguard them as a
reference point that cannot be renounced for
those who style themselves Catholics and who
wish to belong to the ecclesial community.

"The Church considers, therefore, that she
can proclaim her convictions on the family,
certain that she is rendering a service to all
men. She would betray man if she passed over
in silence her message on the family. Be sure,

therefore, that you are sowing good whenever you announce the Good News about the family with freedom, humility, and love.

"May our families be strong with the strength of God; may the divine law, grace and love guide them; may the face of the earth be renewed in them and for them."

A Proposal

While the universe is a place where people are often in conflict, or offend and hurt each other, the example of the mutual love of two spouses is a most stupendous reality.

The sacred author, Sirach, commented: "With three things I am delighted,

for they are pleasing to the LORD and to men: Harmony among brethren, friendship among neighbors,

and the mutual love of husband and wife" (Sirach 25:1).

Here is the final thought which is similar to a proposal:

We cannot tear pages from the book of our life, but we can turn the page and begin to live as though it were the first day of our wedding. Spring begins with the first flower, the day with the first ray of light, the night with the first star. A stream begins with the first drop, a fire with the first spark and love with the first dream; but concord between husband and wife and their spiritual harmony can begin with this first and renewed proposal: live joyfully the totality of love!

Daughters of St. Paul

MASSACHUSETTS
50 St. Paul's Ave., Jamaica Plain, Boston, MA 02130; **617-522-8911.**
172 Tremont Street, Boston, MA 02111; **617-426-5464; 617-426-4230.**
NEW YORK
78 Fort Place, Staten Island, NY 10301; **212-447-5071; 212-447-5086.**
59 East 43rd Street, New York, NY 10017; **212-986-7580.**
625 East 187th Street, Bronx, NY 10458; **212-584-0440.**
525 Main Street, Buffalo, NY 14203; **716-847-6044.**
NEW JERSEY
Hudson Mall—Route 440 and Communipaw Ave.,
   Jersey City, NJ 07304; **201-433-7740.**
CONNECTICUT
202 Fairfield Ave., Bridgeport, CT 06604; **203-335-9913.**
OHIO
2105 Ontario Street (at Prospect Ave.), Cleveland, OH 44115;
   216-621-9427.
25 E. Eighth Street, Cincinnati, OH 45202; **513-721-4838; 513-421-5733.**
PENNSYLVANIA
1719 Chestnut Street, Philadelphia, PA 19103; **215-568-2638.**
VIRGINIA
1025 King Street, Alexandria, VA 22314; **703-683-1741; 703-549-3806.**
FLORIDA
2700 Biscayne Blvd., Miami, FL 33137; **305-573-1618.**
LOUISIANA
4403 Veterans Memorial Blvd., Metairie, LA 70002; **504-887-7631;
   504-887-0113.**
1800 South Acadian Thruway, P.O. Box 2028, Baton Rouge, LA 70821;
   504-343-4057; 504-381-9485.
MISSOURI
1001 Pine Street (at North 10th), St. Louis, MO 63101; **314-621-0346;
   314-231-1034.**
ILLINOIS
172 North Michigan Ave., Chicago, IL 60601; **312-346-4228; 312-346-3240.**
TEXAS
114 Main Plaza, San Antonio, TX 78205; **512-224-8101; 512-224-0938.**
CALIFORNIA
1570 Fifth Ave., San Diego, CA 92101; **619-232-1442.**
46 Geary Street, San Francisco, CA 94108; **415-781-5180.**
WASHINGTON
2301 Second Ave., Seattle, WA 98121; **206-623-1320; 206-623-2234.**
HAWAII
1143 Bishop Street, Honolulu, HI 96813; **808-521-2731.**
ALASKA
750 West 5th Ave., Anchorage, AK 99501; **907-272-8183.**

CANADA
3022 Dufferin Street, Toronto 395, Ontario, Canada.
GREAT BRITAIN
199 Kensington High Street, London W8 6BA, England.
133 Corporation Street, Birmingham B4 6PH, England.
5A-7 Royal Exchange Square, Glasgow G1 3AH, Scotland.
82 Bold Street, Liverpool L1 4HR, England.
AUSTRALIA
58 Abbotsford Rd., Homebush, N.S.W. 2140, Australia.